# Write Now!

*From head to read in 90 days*!

The simple way to write your book in 90 days.

**Lisett Guevara, MSIE**

**Jim Gulnick, MBA**

90daysoulmate.com, LLC

New Jersey, USA

Write Now! *From head to read in 90 days!*

Write Now!            *From head to read in 90 days!*

Copyright © 2017 by Lisett M. Guevara, MSIE

James R. Gulnick, MBA

ALL RIGHTS RESERVED

No part of this publication may be reproduced, stored in a retrieval system, or transmitted in any form or by any means, electronic, mechanical, photocopying, recording, scanning or otherwise, except as permitted under Section 107 or 108 of the United States Copyright Act of 1976, without the prior written permission of the author.

Limitation of Liability / Disclaimer of Warranty: While the publisher and authors have put forth their best efforts in preparing this book, that does not make any representation of warranties regarding the accuracy or completeness of the contents of this book and We specifically disclaim any implied warranty of merchantability or fitness for a particular purpose. The advice and strategies contained herein may not be suitable for your situation. Neither the publisher nor the authors shall hold any responsibility for damages, including but not limited to special, incidental, consequential, or any other form of damage.

Cover Design: Rafael Guevara

Photography: Amer Chaundhry, New Jersey, www.amer-fotografia.net

1st Edition: U.S.A (2017)

www.90daybook.com

Editing: Carolina González

www.carolinagonzalezarias.com/

ISBN: 978-1-941435-06-9

Editorial:

90daysoulmate.com, LLC

Write Now! *From head to read in 90 days!*

## Dedication

To Irene, Jessica and Alfredo, for being a part of our work by supporting us in our guidance of others to document their heritage.

For the patience and acceptance of our time spent in front of our computers and your understanding the reasons for the loss of those moments of family time.

We trust that you too will leave a beautiful legacy that helps others.

And simply for believing in us...

We love you, Lisett & Jim

Write Now! *From head to read in 90 days!*

# Prologue ...........................................................................................11
## Writing your book in 90 days ...............................................11
## The good writer ....................................................................16

# Chapter I ...........................................................................19
## Knowledge generating techniques ....................................19
## Getting to know your inspiration ......................................19
## Determining your passion .................................................21
## Getting to know your needs ..............................................25

# Chapter II ..........................................................................31
## Deciding what to write .......................................................31
## Define your competencies and knowledge .......................33

# Chapter III .........................................................................37
## What is your legacy ............................................................37

# Chapter IV .........................................................................41
## How to organize your ideas ...............................................41
1. Chronological order ......................................................42
2. Technical order .............................................................42
3. Category order .............................................................43
4. By gender, age, or groups ............................................43
5. By themes or events ....................................................44
## Taking action on your ideas ..............................................44

# Chapter V ..........................................................................51
## Determine your resources .................................................51

# Chapter VI .........................................................................59
## Who is your reader? ...........................................................59

# Chapter VII ........................................................................67
## Connecting to your audience .............................................67

# Chapter VIII .......................................................................75
## Type of Text .........................................................................75
## Academic .............................................................................75
## Journalistic ..........................................................................76
## Technical, instructional, scientific ....................................77
## Literary ................................................................................78
## Fiction ..................................................................................79
## Nonfiction ............................................................................81
## Drafting/Layout ...................................................................81

  Editing .................................................................................. 83

# Chapter IX .......................................................................... 87
  **Cover design** ...................................................................... 87
  **Images** ................................................................................. 88
  **Titles & Subtitles** ............................................................. 89
  **Author Bio** ......................................................................... 96
  **Back cover and spine** ..................................................... 97
  **Type of covers** ............................................................... 100

# Chapter X ........................................................................... 103
  **Registering your copyright** ........................................ 103
  **Getting an ISBN** ............................................................ 104

# Chapter XI .......................................................................... 109
  **Publishing your book** .................................................. 109

# Chapter XII ......................................................................... 115
  **Establishing your 90 day plan** .................................. 115
  **Day 5: Develop your 90 day plan** ............................. 117
  **Day 10: Who is your reader?** .................................... 117
  **Days 11-12: Define your legacy, Connect your skills with your book, and What resources do you have?** ......................................... 117
  **Day 14: Determine your limits** ................................ 119
  **Day 15: Determine your target reader/market** .................. 120
  **Day 17-18: Match emotional style of book with reader and Develop attraction list** ..................................... 121
  **Day 19: Select your style of writing and Basic structure of the content** ............................................................. 121
  **Day 20-30: Develop chapters, revise, and analyze, and Review content and organization** ............................................ 122
  **Day 30-60: Develop chapters, revise, and analyze, and Review content and organization (continue moving forward)** ............... 122
  **Day 60: Send to review organization and content** ................. 123
  **Day 65: Send to review spelling and grammar** ..................... 123
  **Day 70-75: Send corrections and reorganization of chapters if needed, Check for need of revision, and Send to two friends for feedback** ........................................................................ 123
  **Day 78: Prepare the cover concept and Select images and title** ............................................................................... 124
  **Day 80: Prepare cover and biography for publication** ............ 125
  **Day 85: Submit and establish copyright** ............................. 125

**Day 86: Secure an ISBN and Convert ISBN to bar code for cover with pricing information**......................................................................125
**Day 87: Register on POD website to publish and Upload cover, content, and description** ........................................................126
**Day 90: Choose sales channels** ..........................................................126

Get ready to Write Now!

## Prologue

## Writing your book in 90 days

The delaying of things for "later" is that dark and gloomy area where lives "never again". This is a place where the feeling of something waiting is generated, which may be motivating for some, but for others, only frustration stalks. Something is in there, but it is dark and gloomy. Like a two-faced bear in its lair, delay looms with its soft fur enticing and embracing us in our moment of procrastination. However, when we realize we haven't worked on what we hoped to achieve, delay's claws and jagged teeth are revealed. Each day we make the choice of either facing our monster or shutting the door to ignore and hope it goes away.

The "later" is also the place where time does not exist; it is an infinite place where we put all those things that we think are not important. The "later" is sometimes called the "after I do this", "when I have time", or "now is not the time". In short, "later" has many names, but it is all the same place. That place is where we accumulate and stockpile things not unlike that room of the house where you hoard that which you do not believe important and that which you do not use, but do not cast off because you think that someday you may need it. It builds up until one day when you try to open the door it spills out all around.

We want you to imagine this room, the "later", where we keep a lot of dreams, projects, agreements, plans, commitments until we are waiting to be rescued from the need to put them into action. We may secretly think someone will do them for us, we will win the lottery, or they will happen by themselves through positive thoughts and prayer. Maybe we are simply waiting for the perfect day where time, responsibilities, and planets agree - the syzygy of our lives in perfect harmonic alignment.

To more accurately visualize the scene, imagine that you are running down the hall in front of that room. You need some things that you know are in that room, but do not have time to go and look for them. Then, you simply walk from one side of the house to the other, complaining and lamenting to yourself about not having what you want. So you go out into the street and keep looking for that which your house already holds, doing everything you can in order to not to have to enter that room and confront the great monster "later" that keeps all your ideas and projects out of your reach.

Before entering the practical 90-day plan, you need to free yourself from those bonds that entrap you in a place of inaction. That moment of inertia which paralyzes your creativity, in which doubts, regrets, fears and complaints are jumbled up in your head, perpetually debating how you came to find yourself in this situation. It is a game in which the mind acts as an alleged victim as a broken system robs you of creativity, innovation, action, and makes you a robot just going through the motions of everyday life.

At this point you may be making excuses to yourself, saying things such as, "Because I have five children to support, two jobs, a dog, a company, debt, an illness, and on top of it all, school and work…" In the end, you could write thousands of sentences that support your inaction and obligate you to a mundane routine. We sometimes work harder to avoid the work that we avoid than the work itself that would be needed to achieve what we avoided in the first place. This self-talk haunts your mind and it uses these excuses to not allow you to escape you daily life. And, if you were able to break yourself free and enter **a place of creative action and not just routine action,** it may be the exact place in which you may discover yourself.

Is it for this reason that you flee? "Too scared to discover me."

We could explain many techniques and methods for managing time. We could spend hours talking with you to try and motivate you. But, the first step you need to take is to ***make a commitment*** to yourself ***to have the discipline*** to follow the instructions that we will offer you here in this book.

*"Commitment and Discipline"*

When we are training the groups in our seminars on how to write a book in 90 days, we are amazed by the wealth of valuable and marvelous information that exists in the minds of participants. Vibrant information dances and flows in their thoughts and words. However, converting this into an understandable form that can be presented clearly and concisely to the public becomes a difficult task indeed. We have found many artists, romantics, philosophers, psychologists, and even technicians who are in love with their ideas. Most have been unable to follow through with the process of documenting their beautiful concepts and respected lessons for easy absorption by the reader.

It is just a question of starting. It is that simple. You sit with a fresh mind to develop content; let the mind flow without having to force it. **When the pleasure of what you do takes over your consciousness, your creativity and innovation emerge so that your ideas are assembled, packaged, labeled, and transported to the hand of the consumer.**

Remember that the only person capable of vanquishing unproductivity is you. When you truly believe that you possess worthwhile information and ideas as well as believe that you are skilled in the ability to connect your knowledge with your experience, skills and unique talents, is when your belief will give you the energy and power to create. *If you do not believe in yourself, you cannot create.*

## *"Belief precipitates Creativity"*

It all comes down to beliefs. Maybe at this time your thoughts and ideas are not totally clear. They may start to quarrel among themselves. Spiritual beliefs challenge the scientific evidence, and emotional intuition is at odds with what appears to be rational concepts. Overall, what you know in your heart and mind is debated daily as thoughts struggle in pursuit of reason. Indecision, and tentative beliefs generate a paralysis of creativity in your life.

It is amazing how we have realized when *coaching* a person who is looking to create things, whether business, family, projects, children's books, that the mind and heart have a deep internal struggle that blocks and prevents him or her from moving forward, producing a self-sabotage that discourages and even moves toward a state of greater unconsciousness to avoid having to deal with the large struggle around what he or she should believe.

Speaking of belief, why not start by calling yourself 'author'? Imagine at this time going to an event and meeting new people. Try to practice introducing yourself as the author of a bestseller, even if you have not yet published your first book. What feeling does it give you? You may be afraid, anxious and feel that is a delusion. An author or writer need not have a college degree nor is he or she required to have a license, certification, degrees, credentials, etc. So it all begins with believing in you, <u>beginning to feel the responsibility of being a writer.</u> Why do we use the word 'responsibility'? Because the fact that your ideas are published, read and followed by others must engender the responsibility for creating good content, information that promotes values that help people, which increases knowledge. That is why we stress the importance of accountability. If you felt comfortable at the beginning when I said that anyone can be a writer; yes, it's true, but being a **good writer** is something else entirely.

We really want to become good writers, creative people who can make contributions to the world, to society. We want you to be able to leave a legacy that your children, grandchildren, family, and society can appreciate, because you are unique. Only you have that special mix of experience, skill and knowledge; only you have lived through unique situations that can help others learn to avoid needless suffering and enjoy themselves. Evaluate all that you have, determine the reason you came to this planet, and think about the emptiness that that can generate in you, on this path that is life, if not leaving a mark.

### The good writer

This method that we have created and implemented to help build the process of creating your book does not guarantee the quality of the content. But do not be discouraged because when you use this method and there is a commitment, responsibility and discipline, you can connect with yourself, and that connection to the power flow will enable the quality of the information. Of course, you must follow the instructions that we introduce. If you do, you can bet you will be one of those good writers.

We not only want to motivate you to accomplish your goal of writing your book, but also make you aware that the role of providing help and benefits to many others through knowledge and is a responsibility that rests in your hands.

Generating knowledge involves several techniques that will be described in this book, so that you can find a method that works for you. This does not mean that we want to put a straitjacket on your creativity; on the contrary, we want to give you the necessary tools to be able to freely enhance your style, and discover your art. Many famous artists and writers did not follow guidelines, or techniques; inspiration just carried them away, and that inspiration was the engine for creation. In other instances, they developed their skills through learning and preparation as you are doing now.

Your inspiration may lead you through the labyrinths of fiction, which does not mean they are not making contributions to knowledge of society, because through this fiction, fantasy, many geniuses managed to develop great discoveries. Think about it, there are no limits if you see this opportunity as the therapy you need in to bring it all together - your mind, your heart, your soul and your keyboard.

**Notes**

## Chapter I

## Knowledge generating techniques

### Getting to know your inspiration

Inspiration is the muse that frees your soul. It becomes the moment when intuition is mixed with reason, like two musical instruments that harmonize their notes to create a song. When reason acts alone, inspiration can be very mechanical, very basic and unattractive. In that moment in which logic gives way to intuition, to that part of our mind that does not have a logical process, but simply exists, it explodes, shoots colors everywhere, and then gently shapes reason and is converted into perfect inspiration.

*Discovering what inspires you* will be the first task you must perform, because through this you can obtain the energy you are going use to charge your batteries during this adventure. You must visualize a place in your mind where intuition and reason are waiting for you. There you will sit with them to discuss the topic you are passionate about and through doing this you will connect your mind to the fountain of knowledge.

When I talk about the fountain of knowledge, I refer to that extraordinary moment when spontaneous ideas come to you, ones that make you smile and say, "Yes !, that is it, there is the way." Usually, at this time, intuition welcomes you and gives you a pat on the back, while reason takes a baseball bat and destroys everything, telling you that already exists, makes not logical sense, to stop dreaming and just walk away.

The fountain of knowledge is a key moment that can ignite us, if we practice and take time to think, feel and connect. As human beings we have the left hemisphere of reason and the right of intuition, but also there exists a place in the center of our brain that connects the two. This is where we should focus our attention and put it to work.

To find out more about what things generate inspiration we are going to relate it to your passion because when you discover what things you are passionate about, you realize that when passion is present, inspiration flows naturally.

In the following practical exercise you will fill out a form, which will be your guide through this adventure. Answer the following questions, taking the time to think and be honest with your answers.

## Determining your passion

1) What activity do you perform in which you lose track of the time?

2) What would you be willing to do without ever being paid a penny for it?

3) At this point, what would choosing to do it do to the rest of your life?

4) If you died and were given the opportunity to come back, what would you return to do?

**Notes**

5) What activity triggers creativity and get you excited?

6) Remember and write some moments that brought you joy, made you jump, that energized you and made you happy?

Once you have answered each question, looking for a highlighter and mark the key words in each sentence, words or ideas that are repeated in the answers. This will help for the following exercises in the book.

**Notes**

## Getting to know your needs

Why is it important to know your needs? Because they have the magical power of making or breaking any dream or project if you do not align with them. Needs, according to Maslow table, range from the most basic to the highest, but they all have a lot of power in our lives.

If I am working on something that does not meet one of my needs, it is likely that I will do it with very little motivation, with little optimism. That situation is not good to sit down and create and even worse for the generating of knowledge. Like a wise saying says: "Love with unfulfilled hunger does not last." It sounds unromantic, it's true, but it's very raw and real. If my needs are not met, I cannot have that inspiration, the ability to generate good information. By this, I do not mean that I have to have my financial needs covered to find inspiration. No, it's not about that; as unique human beings, everyone has different levels of need.

Although they have been characterized and classified by some psychologists, one person's needs can be very different from others. You've seen wonderful street artists whose inspiration is not diminished by their need for food, clothing, etc. For them, their needs are different and inspiration and passion are nourished by contact with nature, talking to people, looking at the landscapes, children, animals. In the end, they found their fountain of inspiration and they connect to it and create. If you took those artists and limited their freedom to do these things, the ability to feel the world around them, if you locked them up, would their inspiration and creativity still thrive?

It is important that you find out for yourself what these needs are, those that can give you the peace of mind to follow your path, those without which you would be out of control. Remember that this process of writing a book, no matter what specialty you want to write about, is closely related to your being who you really are and expressing what you want to express. Therefore it is very important to do the exercises, because they allow you to meet and discover those skills, experiences, knowledge and attitudes that make you and the book you will write unique.

I want to emphasize the discovery of your needs, as well the power they have to destroy a project, also that they have the power to push you to go out in search of whatever it takes to meet them. When you wake up every morning and leave, whether to work, to school, to the park, to drink a coffee or just to breathe, behind it there is a need for your body, your mind and/or your soul. When we do not know what those needs are, we can be working on what we call the middle ground, where we are neither reaching 100% for a specific need, nor 0%. When you are on this middle ground some things you do will meet your needs halfway, sometimes not, and then not knowing what they are leads to mediocrity, lack of motivation, and no connection to the fountain can occur. When creating your masterpiece, you will have sentences, ideas or words that do not fit, do not harmonize, putting you in the group of authors who write something, but they do not get readers to follow or understand or appreciate the content.

Speaking of appreciation, this is another key point that you must discover on your journey to transform your life through writing your book. Many of our clients who have attended our seminars or received personalized services relate how writing the book allowed them to transform an important part of their lives, because writing and our method led them to discover an area that they did not know and that was the key to meet the muse that connected them directly to the fountain and lead to the so-called "intellectual orgasm " of which we always talk.

**Notes**

I invite you to do the following exercise and, as always, be very open in your answers:

- Write a list of five needs that you consider important to you.
- Sort the list from most important to least important.

| Need | Position from 1-5 |
|---|---|
|  |  |
|  |  |
|  |  |
|  |  |
|  |  |

Once you have filled out the box, think a little about how that need could be affecting you, for example, that which you placed in the number 2 position in the previous exercise. What need is holding you back from achieving everything you wish to achieve. Also think about what needs you now have covered that make you happy and relate it with the last question of the exercise. It is important to write these thoughts, for these will be invaluable information for the development of your book and inserting it into the right market, thereby reaching your target audience.

There are people who have decided to write a book for personal or family use, writing a biography, a story of family, etc. Others have chosen to write how to books for business, cooking, self-help or they write history or fiction novels, etc. Whatever the topic you want to develop it is important that what you are going to write relates, in one way or another to who you are, because you are speaking from your knowledge, generating knowledge through your experience, your skills, and for that you must have knowledge and clarity about whatever it is. That way, you will produce a quality book and you have the image of a great, unique, authentic writer.

By following these steps you will see that at the end of this book not only do you have enough material to write a great book, but to position it and design it from the perspective of a reader who really enjoys your work. This is a product to be designed with extreme caution; from the moment of conception, it should be planned, prepared and created with great care in every detail to make this a work of art that people want to read.

**Notes**

## Chapter II

### Deciding what to write

Our mind transports us through endless ideas and possibilities, allowing us on occasion to stick to a single path. It is normal to go through that process as we determine the specific topic to write. We can be transported by our passion as well as what we believe is the best idea we have ever had, even if, in all actuality, it is not.

We find ourselves in that place of not knowing what it is that we want that transitional moment of sorting ideas to be, but this is not a place that we should linger and dwell. In all the experiences we have worked through, as a couple, in business and in life, when people do not know what they really want, they find their energies, efforts and resources depleted, leaving them with a bad taste in their mouth that stifles their ability to advance.

In our seminars we always put forth the example of imagining a highway in which each person should know where he or she is going. Each of them has doubts about whether to go ahead, slow down, turn off or even reverse. What would happen? On the one hand it slows down other people, congests the traffic and could heightens the risk of crashing, suffering an unfortunate accident, wasting time, money, and creating undue stress on the other. Just because of not knowing where you are going, not being clear about which path to take, having no decisiveness and certainty in the decision and just moving on.

In the same way, this happens when we have a project, a job, a relationship, a family and start writing a book. Of course, it is not easy to know from the beginning what you want, but that is when you should take the time to figure it out - before even getting into the driver's seat. It is that moment when you determine where you want to go, what route you will take, and what time you intend to arrive, considering setbacks. That is why this moment of *not knowing* you must decide to make a fleeting place, rather than transforming it into a habit of making excuses not to drive to your destination because you do not know where you should be, you do not have the time or it is more comfortable living in the *I don't know*.

In any situation in which you place yourself, there are always three options: *yes, no* and *I don't know*. *I don't know* is not a comfortable place, as you are in a position of being unable to make a choice and this can be much more costly than *yes* or *no*. But one should keep in mind that making decisions under pressure, under stress, or with little information can lead us to failure as well so decision-making definitely has its nuances.

The first decision you must make is whether you really have the commitment to yourself to write that book you always imagine. If you take this step up front, you will minimize the constant damage of *later* or living in the *I don't know*.

Once you know where you are going and when you want to arrive (remember that the timeline has already been established with our 90 day method), you eliminate two major variables, so you can continue the journey. Now select the best course that enables you to minimize the delay, with which you make best use of your resources and do not have to make detours, do any braking, experience any setbacks or cause any accidents.

## Define your competencies and knowledge

Knowing what skills you possess is one of the fundamental steps to determining the subject and style of your book. It is important to recognize in what area you have strengths, either by way of study, work, experiences, innate abilities, or by other means.

**Determine the talents, skills, and knowledge that you possess.**

It is important to recognize the difference between these elements; they seem similar, but they are not. Knowledge is knowing something and the skill is knowing how to actually do it.

When we speak of *knowledge* we refer to the acquired theoretical information about a subject, that information learned through reading, training or any means of acquiring knowledge.

Moreover, *skill* is the practical ability to apply the knowledge gained.

In some cases the skills may be innate, because there are people that develop without prior studies, perhaps watching or just trying by trial and error.

When we speak of *talent*, we can say that it is the combination of these two definitions. It joins the ability of the person to understand intelligently how to solve a particular situation with the use of his or her own abilities, skills, knowledge, experience and skills.

Having the meanings of these terms clear in your mind enables you to identify every talent, skill and piece of knowledge that you have, giving you the basics needed to know yourself better and understand the tools you have.

Note the importance of this part of self-analysis, because disregarding the skills that we possess can make that road ahead a very difficult one to navigate. When you really know who you are, you can better understand your weaknesses and strengths. Through this, you can determine which areas you need to improve and those that you can use to your advantage more easily.

When people recognize their talents, they can become superheroes more quickly and easily. I know people with an innate ability to connect with others when they communicate and sell anything, because they have that gift that makes them unique when it comes to presenting a product or service. Such people can go far in the area because of this ability. Just knowing what talent you have and ardently believing in your talent gives you the potential you need to succeed.

A simple way to do this analysis is by recalling the activities you find easy and which others recognize that you perform well.

Another way is to evaluate the knowledge acquired in all your years of life and experience. Some people have twenty years working as assistants or technicians in a machine shop and do not recognize all the knowledge they have in the area of mechanical, electrical and component nor do they realize the amount of training that they have received, etc.

Evaluate yourself. I know that it seems meticulous to consider your whole career, looking at all of this knowledge, talent and experience, but this allows you to paint a full picture of who you really are and what you possess.

**Notes**

# Chapter III

## What is your legacy

Not everyone knows the mission they have to accomplish on this planet; some just speculate; others are already sure what it is. The point is to know what to do and how you can leave that footprint that can transcend time, regardless of whether you are alive or dead. Knowing that legacy we have come to leave on the planet becomes the meaning of life for many people. It is like that personal therapy in which the writer connects with his or her inner self and begins his or her self-discovery through writing.

Remember that in our brain we have a left and right hemisphere; one handles the logical part and the other is more of an artist and improviser. By knowing how to connect these two hemispheres at the time of writing or creating anything, we are transformed into successful beings. That is when we begin to feel that wonderful passion for what we do.

The experiences we have had with those people who we helped write their books using our method have been wonderful, because living this process has allowed them to discover the path to connecting with that valuable knowledge, transforming their lives and those of others. They have discovered wonderful information; they have had a transformation of their writing that has permitted them, in some cases, to realize the very reason that they came to this earth and how to manage their life's mission. It sounds too good to be true, right? Just the simple fact that you are able to put your ideas on paper sparks your creative side that was quite possibly asleep and that under our method it is activated and begins to emerge a overflow with knowledge and information that may become part of your life and allow you to positively influence the lives of many others.

It could be a book of fiction, mystery or perhaps adventure; write what you want; you will always have a special touch to your ideas, your style, the message you want to leave behind in every paragraph, in every topic and every story.

Knowing that message you want to share will increase the commitment that you feel to yourself and your reader, to deliver a quality and attractive manuscript that captures the mind and the heart of everyone.

We know it is not easy to organize ideas; more so if this is first time you want to write a book. The important thing is to follow the method with order and discipline, as there will be many ideas, manuscripts, drawings, graphics, paragraphs on your desktop, and how to organize them in a logical and easy to understand way is part of the tools that we are going to provide.

We recommend that you take the time to describe your great gift, the knowledge you control and the experiences you have. By linking this information you can better visualize your life mission. It is no coincidence that you are reading this book and much less that you feel a commitment to yourself and to your future readers.

We recommend that you fill in this chart, as it will help you discover that which is your legacy.

| # | What are your innate gifts? | With whom do you desire to share them? |
|---|---|---|
| 1 | | |
| 2 | | |
| 3 | | |
| 4 | | |
| 5 | | |

**Notes**

# Chapter IV

## How to organize your ideas

We know that anxiety you feel when ideas become a whirlwind competing with each other, and revealing only doubt as to which of them is the best. Establishing the importance of the topic on which you are focused lets you discover which is the most important, <u>for the reader, to the market, or just for you.</u> This fear that we have when wanting to know how to sort, classify and structure ideas transforms itself into a compelling read for others.

The mind game is challenging, because a wealth of knowledge and information are in search of order, which enables flow and assimilation. This is where sometimes we lack the tools or methods for weaving and linking these ideas.

Imagine you are participating in a seminar where the speaker has lots of valuable knowledge, but maybe the thrill of connecting with the audience makes him jump from one point to another without a logical order. You may end the session with a highly motivated audience, energized, but ultimately they do not leave with anything in their hands that actually allows them to put into action that which they have learned.

This can happen with a book as well. Everything depends on the <u>type of text</u> you want to write, <u>to which the public will be directed,</u> and <u>the purpose</u> of your book. Your ideas can be very interesting, but if you lack the ability to transform them into a familiar language to captivate the target audience, you are simply creating a manuscript for your own use.

## 1. Chronological order

When we write stories, novels, true events, bios, etc., the chronological order is essential for the reader to understand where it comes from and where it goes. In some cases, you can start at the end, like in the movies, to make a journey through time from the bottom to the top or vice versa, but in those cases you must be careful that you are not losing your reader along the way. It is important to maintain control over the management of verb conjugation (walked vs. had walked) and time and date references so that people can understand where they are in the story.

## 2. Technical order

If your book is a method, a manual, instructions or another practical document to achieve a specific goal, you must order the pieces from the starting point to the end product. In this case, creating process maps, mind maps, flow charts, etc. will allow you to have an overall picture of your idea in one plane and in turn fill in the information for each section. Through care in the flow of arrows from entry to exit, you will be able to have a better idea of how to organize and construct the chapters of your book.

## 3. Category order

For example, if you want to write a book of recipes, you can sort by category, whether types of dishes (appetizers, desserts, salads, etc.) or cultures, countries, colors or sizes. If that which you desire to write is well organized in terms of category, you will be able to convert it in a way that makes it easy to organize ideas and develop each category.

When developing the first category you can find a pattern that allows you to standardize information for the categories that follow. When you standardize the structure of the information, it facilitates the finding and understanding of that information by the reader using the book.

## 4. By gender, age, or groups

A bit like the previous one, the handling of topics for men, women, children, adolescents, adults, etc., can help to better classify information and set chapters for each gender, simplifying the task for the reader of finding the desired information. Sometimes gender can have subclasses and this allows you to sub-divide the chapters.

## 5. By themes or events

If you find the chronological aspect difficult to manage, you can establish events or themes to play out and develop each theme in full. In this case, first, you determine all the themes and then look for the natural order present within them. You must be careful and organized to avoid confusion. For example, you make reference to a subject or event in an earlier chapter, which is encountered again in a later chapter. You must make several revisions to avoid referring to a point that is another chapter. Usually, these are independent themes. There are cases where people conduct interviews with people and then highlight the messages in each interview. In that case, they organize messages separately to then determine the order of the interviews, as this allows the reader begin to understand messages with certain logic.

## Taking action on your ideas

You can already start developing your ideas and putting them on paper. You will rely a lot on the mental maps where a central idea can open itself up into other ideas, which open up to more ideas and so on. In this way you are establishing the framework for your book.

For example, I cite the case of a person who wants to write a book on handling relationships. In this case the lens or main idea in the center of a paper was placed and from it projected lines types, categories, genders. So the writer could see how their ideas flowed and connected under a scheme, which will then be easier to develop.

This simple example will give you a reference for how to organize your ideas and develop each specific topic.

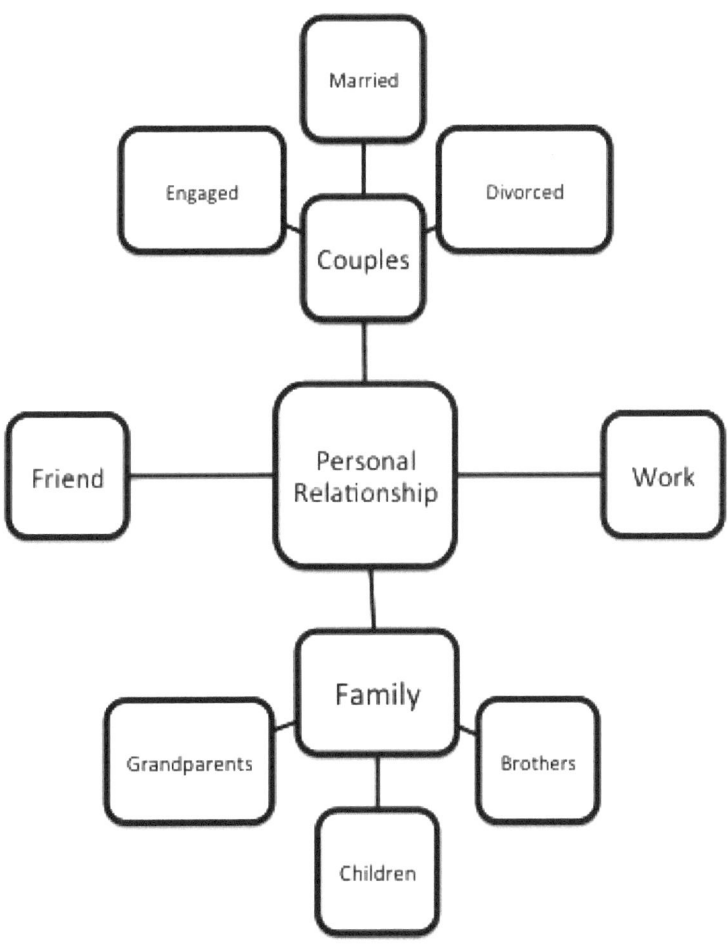

Another example is the *use of process* approach, where you lay out the input- process -output and from there you can go about the process of determining the themes.

| INPUT | PROCESS | OUTPUT |
|---|---|---|
| **Caring for plants** | Prepare the soil | Soil that is ready for planting |
| | Planting | A planted plant |
| | Maintaining | A healthy plant |
| **Plant ailments** | In the leaves | Medications and treatments for the leaves |
| | In the stem | Treatments for the stem |
| | In the root | Treatments for the root |

Here is a blank process template for you to work with and discover if this methodology helps you in structuring your ideas.

| INPUT | PROCESS | OUTPUT |
|---|---|---|
|  |  |  |
|  |  |  |
|  |  |  |
|  |  |  |
|  |  |  |
|  |  |  |
|  |  |  |
|  |  |  |
|  |  |  |

These examples will allow you to better manage ideas and make combinations of methods. By making a mind map you can create steps, timelines; there are no limitations when it comes to establishing methods to organize your book. The important point is to keep it simple and easy to understand for the reader.

Self-help books that teach need to be constructed in a different way than a book on the life of a sports hero. Self-help books contain step-by-step processes whereas biographies may follow a life timeline but are not trying to teach specific skills to the reader. You will find charts, bullet points, numbered sections, and worksheets that are presented for reader interaction throughout this book. *Write Now!* is also used in workshops with participants utilizing the book as a mini-workbook where lessons and examples are mixed with worksheets that are filled out throughout the course.

We like to present our materials as a "seminar-in-a-book" approach to appeal to readers and workshop attendees alike. This allows us to focus on our best approach with our target audience and help them connect to our message through our talents and skills. We are teachers, engineers, authors, businesspeople, and husband and wife. We are formal and informal, creative and logical. Or, at least we'd like to think that we are! ;)

## Notes

Write Now! *From head to read in 90 days!*

# Chapter V

## Determine your resources

I will emphasize here that you need to recognize what resources you possess. When we talk about resources we do not mean just the financial part, but the existence of the ***infinite resources and opportunities*** that often you do not perceive yet that are right there at your fingertips. For some reason, people have limited sight, only seeing the knowledge in their immediate vicinity; letting the plethora of options escape them as said limits cloud their vision.

Here, we will refer to several important resources that will allow you to connect with the opportunities and be better able to sharpen your targeting skills to hit the bull's-eye. When you want to know to which target audience you should aim your book, you should really review the resources at your fingertips, such as:

**1. Relationships:** As a means of unraveling this, consider what people you have around you: coworkers, neighbors, associations, clubs, family, friends, etc. Belonging to a group of any kind can open doors for you immediately. For example, suppose you work as a resident doctor, a salesman, a coach, a bus driver, a housewife, a cafeteria worker, etc. Whatever your activity, there are a number of people who have the same profession; some tasks in common, the same goal. They work in a common environment and therefore have so much valuable experience just waiting there for you.

By knowing what relationships you have, you identify a potential target audience, easily accessible, as you move in the same environment, handle information, you can easily connect with people, either to seek more information or to provide information in common. These groups can become both a source of information and potential readers and followers.

**2. Access to information:** Access to information is a valuable resource, because not only will it help you before you develop your book, but during its drafting, and, even better, after your book is ready. Observe how many accesses to information on the subject you want to develop; limit, shape and adjust the coordinates in your GPS based on that access, as it will be very difficult to develop ideas that require investigation for which access is limited.

Organizing the sources of information at your fingertips will be a great help to you, since it will facilitate the execution of a good marketing strategy to sell your book. Make lists of what you need to know and analyze the opportunity that you have to get that information.

**3. Your public image:** In the world of social media, the public image is becoming more volatile, more sensitive; you can even see that even in the number of followers you have on a social network, but beyond this environment, you have a public image in the workplace, among family, friends, neighbors and in the community. Whatever your profession or trade, this image is how others see you, what characterizes you and what makes people want to read what you write. Whether you have created an image of being assertive, critical, suspicious, ironic, funny, articulate, intelligent, spontaneous, romantic or whatever it might be, that is the way you will project yourself to others.

**4. Distribution and Expansion:** In most cases when we write a book we are looking for it to be read by a large number of people with a reach that is as broad as possible. This requires a lot of resources, but if you really evaluate point 1 about the relationships you have and what circles you move within and your public image, this can give you direction on how to cover more ground than you think.

Imagine that you move into the construction business and your book refers to any technique that can help the workers in this field. The simple fact that you lean on the relationships you have in that environment can lead to the establishment of alliances to achieve distribution of your book locally, nationally and even internationally. The simple analysis of the resources that are your own can succeed in establishing marketing strategies and distribution of your book with little money up front.

An important point here is to establish precisely to what extent you are expanding your market and what you want to achieve, because when developing your book you can include your colleagues on the topic in the book that you are developing and open more doors for you to expand your market.

Sometimes we say that the book is your business card if you are a consultant, psychologist, counselor, etc. Having a book gives you a better image to your customers and society as a whole, and then just having a book out there will be part of your personal and professional *marketing*.

**5. Financial resources:** Remember that every project requires investment and you should be absolutely clear about your ability to invest in the realization of the book. That is perhaps the least of it, as it is the marketing and distribution of said book, which requires more resources.

Set stages, objectives and put in place monthly, quarterly and annual targets regarding where to invest, then you will gradually start seeing yourself recovering that investment. Possibly you take months or even years thinking about writing a book, so why not have the foresight to create a small monthly savings that will allow you in a period of one year to be able to enter this wonderful world of writers

**6. Testimonials:** It is possible that through the relationships you have and the activities you do, there are people who in some way or another you have helped and these become testimonials that become a valuable resource for your book in different ways:

- ✓ Testimonies can become a chapter in your book, which increases credibility.
- ✓ Those statements may involve other people in your book, which will support you in your task of disseminating information.
- ✓ Personal, group or organizational testimony will be necessary support when your book is finished.
- ✓ Real stories attract a lot of public attention, as is seen when a film is based on real events. This type of information generates higher expectations and interest among readers.
- ✓ If your book is fictional you can involve real world people and get them to support your book.

| Areas | Resources | How to Connect them |
|---|---|---|
| Relationships | | |
| Access to Information | | |
| Public Image | | |
| Distribution and Expansion | | |
| Finances | | |
| Testimonies | | |
| | | |

**Notes**

Write Now! *From head to read in 90 days!*

## Chapter VI

### Who is your reader?

Really identifying to whom you are directing your book is essential to refine all of the content, context, form, title, and even the colors and design of the cover. From the beginning you should think carefully about who your reader is, what age range the person is, gender, marital status, occupation, socioeconomic status, interests, and dare to be even more specific and add what emotions and attitudes they may have or in what circumstances the reader who would be interested in your book may be living.

Knowing that emotional part is key, because it is a way to connect with the person who will be interested in your book. Really take a look at what you are writing, how it makes you feel, and to this end you must read what you are writing.

You are not writing the same way to reach someone in a field such of medicine, business or engineering, as you would when speaking to housewives, teenagers or children. When you are clear to whom you are addressing your content, you will be yet more successful in in handling your marketing strategy.

Maybe you decided to write a book for all ages. For example, self-help books usually are not directed to any gender, age or particular profession. If this is your situation, you should just go for a more generic design and content with a neutral cover and a title that appeals to many.

If this is the first book you want to write, do not feel overwhelmed with all of this information as to whether what you write will be for a specific group or its contents will speak to a wider audience. Do not be afraid about whatever decisions you might make with the your first book. When you write the second or third, you will have the opportunity to be more directed toward the many options and resources that you find around you. What's more, you can make your first book a first edition, which means that you can adjust and refine it later and republish it. **When, in your mind, you realize that there is a possibility to improve what you have already accomplished, the inertia of perfection is cast aside, letting you take those risks without fear.**

Clearly describing your reader on paper is essential for development in the course of your book so as not to lose the style and content. Especially when you describe the emotions. Remember that the attractiveness of a book is how it captivates the emotions and the reader's attention. To do this you should consider what possible emotions you can engage in your writing that capture the attention.

You must know what interest a person has in looking for the information in your book; if it is highly technical information, it must be precise. Provide examples, display tables, lists or recipes. If it is a story, you must help the reader visualize rooms and environments very well so that he or she can live in the moment you want to recreate. The interests are closely connected with the circumstances, the emotions, and that should be a springboard from which you can develop and structure the content.

Remember to learn to connect with your reader. You should feel it. You should put yourself in his or her shoes. You must think like him or her. Ask yourself the questions what he or she is possibly doing. You must intelligently slip between the mind and the heart. With that information the necessary link can flourish into a magical writer-reader relationship.

The success of many writers was found with that ability to be intimate with the reader through books. When a reader is able to recognize the author's thoughts in a very raw and real way from just reading a paragraph it establishes the link, which will then be difficult to break.

Create an intellectual-emotional connection with your reader. Dare to share that which makes you unique and you will connect with many in a natural way.

Sometimes people who have read our first book <u>90 Day Soulmate, that's the story of love...</u> tell us that in some chapters, while reading, they can feel our voice in their minds. That tells us that as we are writing a very distinctive type of reading, custom, you could say, while creating a brand and our own style in our books.

Here we give you a guide for you describe your reader, but do not let that limit you. Be as open as possible:

1. Ages (from-to)

2. Gender

3. Profession or trade.

4. Socio-economic level




5. Status




6. Interests, hobbies.

7. Emotions, attitudes




8. Life circumstances and necessities




Here write any other notes that make your audience special or unique – things that make them very identifiable. If you were looking at them, talking with them, smelling them, arguing with them, or laughing with them, what would be the context and therefor the things that make them tick.

**Notes**

Write Now! *From head to read in 90 days!*

## Chapter VII

### Connecting to your audience

As mentioned above, writing your book will become your personal therapy. It will let you feel that intellectual orgasm that we like to enjoy when we are writing. As writers, we are going to connect with you from a place of passion and maybe a little humor as well. There are three topics that most people like to read, listen to or watch, and there are subjects that produce joy and laughter; topics that produce pleasure, discord, emotion, suspense, maybe ... orgasms and/or topics that produce peace, tranquility, love.

To connect with your audience you must manipulate the energies and emotions in each sentence, each chapter. You must learn to generate interest, to close a chapter in a way that invites the reader to the next, so that they cannot put your book down. You have to capture the attention of that reader and the best way to do this is to know yourself the best and then know your reader.

Why do we say, "know yourself the best"? ***Because if you do not know what you have, you cannot know what you have to offer.*** Whether you are a happy or sad person, recognizing the emotion, which characterizes you, allows you to be authentic in your writing and the reader will, in turn, trust your information. Thus, you can create information from the heart and the skills you possess.

Let us share an experience we had in a seminar where one of the participants, when performing this exercise to connect with the public, found that he connects much better and writes beautiful verses, poems, stories when he is sad and melancholy. This state gives him the ability to create beautiful content that moves the emotions of anyone. In the midst of the seminar, this person read works that he had created during a separation, after the death of a family member, after the loss of a job, and these works showed this great ability to connect with the emotions through words in a very unique way.

It is important to discover who you are, what skills and competencies you have. Once you get this, you can take what you have and connect with the reader. We have even seen cases of people who have an aptitude for criticism or sarcasm, who by using these techniques, discovered that something that could be considered a negative personality trait could become an opportunity to connect with others. Through this unique talent for sarcasm, this individual created that sweet and sour taste in writing that really captivates an audience.

Find the elements that characterize and connect you with the kind of reader that you are pursuing. It will help you discover the writing style with which your book can stand out from the crowd. Look carefully at the skills you have, those natural skills that you knew you had from an early age, the ones that really made you stand out among your peers. Also, make note of those skills that people recognize in you when you received comments or compliments regarding a task that you completed all by yourself. Once you have your natural skills inventory along with those recognized by others, build your list of acquired knowledge: courses, studies, experiences, books read, films seen, all that information that you have absorbed over time.

In previous exercises, you discovered your passion. Search your notes and incorporate this into the table we are going to provide below. Once you have completed at least five lines of the first four columns, begin to fill the last one, which refers to what your reader will desire to get out of your book. This last column is the key, there you can develop sentences, ideas, keywords about what your reader is looking for in your book. Once you have your box full, continue to stress the keywords that are common between columns, while analyzing which elements you can add that would complement your information. The analysis of this exercise is crucial, because it allows you to set a style with which you feel comfortable, that which makes you unique, and with this you will create an intimate relationship with your reader.

At this point we are tearing up with joy, because this is the most revealing part where everyone will see the doors of opportunity opening wide; here you really begin to see the infinite resources, answers to all the questions. This is where needs meets with resources and intellect connects with emotion.

Once you select keywords, you can determine the writing style to use. What remains is to put it into action with so little standing between you and the writing of each chapter. Each idea will be transformed into content.

For this exercise we include a previous example that will serve as a guide. Once you understand the exercise well, make your own analysis in the next empty table.

**Tip: Use blank space wherever you find it to scratch notes, ideas, pictures, or play tic-tac-toe. It is your book to use in the way you see fit to seed creativity and develop structure. Second hint – the rest of this page is intentionally blank to see how you use it. ☺**

## Determine your competencies and how best to use them to connect with others.

| TALENTS, NATURAL ABILITIES | ABILITIES OBTAINED FROM OTHERS | ACADEMIC KNOWLEDGE AND EXPERIENCE | YOUR PASSION | WHAT DOES YOUR READER DESIRE |
|---|---|---|---|---|
| **Drawing, Coloring** | Drawing | Psychology Professor | Music | Drawing |
| **Arts & Crafts** | Party planning | **Child Therapist** | Drawing | Entertain-ment |
| **Fictional Story-Telling** | Social | Graphite Drawing | **Playing with kids** | Learning |
| **Playing Team Sports** | Extrovert | Theater | Organizing events | Colors |
| **Playing the piano** | Cooking | Reading books of higher learning | Playing the piano | Fun/Passing the time |

*Example of a person who should write children's books.*

**Analysis:** If you look at the highlighted words on the previous page, the references to drawing and accelerated learning knowledge, and the ability to tell fictional stories, you will realize that the most likely choice in style would be children's books with many drawings. Perhaps this individual could develop a distinct style of graphite drawing to be used in illustrations while incorporating elements of his or her professional education. With this example, you can establish an organizational pattern of your competencies, allowing you to better create a path to connect with others.

## Determine your competencies and how best to use them to connect with others.

| TALENTS, NATURAL ABILITIES | ABILITIES OBTAINED FROM OTHERS | ACADEMIC KNOWLEDGE AND EXPERIENCE | YOUR PASSION | WHAT DOES YOUR READER DESIRE |
|---|---|---|---|---|
|  |  |  |  |  |
|  |  |  |  |  |
|  |  |  |  |  |
|  |  |  |  |  |
|  |  |  |  |  |
|  |  |  |  |  |

Write Now! *From head to read in 90 days!*

# Chapter VIII

## Type of Text

There are many ways to classify manuscripts. In general, we want to present you with the simplest possible way in order to reach that moment of classifying content to obtain a copyright and registration code in the international numbering system for books (ISBN).

- **Academic**
- **Journalistic**
- **Technical, instructional, scientific**
- **Literary**
    - **Fiction**
    - **Nonfiction**

## Academic

This type of manuscript is the result of research that allows you to communicate knowledge in certain areas of academia. Generally, these works are used in teaching and research activities in colleges, universities and any academic institution, as a foundation or supplement for any particular subject.

Theses, reports, research projects, summaries, etc., fall into this category of writing that requires some special structure and rules (citations, references, footnotes, etc.) that make your writing a rather specialized task.

Usually this type of text requires an exhaustive review by specialists, both in the topics covered and in the research methodology, before approval. If the topic is sufficiently impactful, transcending academic interests perhaps recognized publishers could give it the support it needs when placing it on the market.

## Journalistic

Journalistic manuscripts are designed within the guidelines of the journalism profession with the overall objective of informing and guiding the reader. While the newspaper articles are written to be published in various media outlets in the form of news, interviews, features, stories, etc., journalistic manuscripts, in many cases, have become best sellers on a global level. For example, the novel In Cold Blood by Truman Capote began, in many ways, what is called New Journalism. Capote mixed facts from a murder case with interviews of people to create an arguably imaginative retelling of the story.

Author Hunter S. Thompson joined Hell's Angels in order to bring to light societal fraudulence through first hand experience in what became known as gonzo journalism. Stories in this style are written first-person narrative without any suggestion of objectivity and many times include the author in the story.

Lastly, Ernest Hemingway used a direct journalistic approach perhaps as honed during his early years as a reporter for The Kansas City Star. He is short, to the point, and rich in the use of simple yet robust language for the masses to easily understand. His style periodically includes short journeys from third- to first-person narratives depending upon the need of the day.

Such texts require in-depth research using reporting and interviewing techniques. In order to give the book substance, the writer is required to use language that allows the manuscript to transcend its purely informative mission and its innate characteristics, to be sufficiently attractive enough to entertain the reader. They can either be closely tied to the facts or loosely based but appearing to be works of non-fiction based on reality. This style gives the impression that the story told is real and in many cases is truly factual without departure.

## Technical, instructional, scientific

There are books that touch on specific topics such as those in a particular field of knowledge like science and technology. Generally they are aimed at a specific audience, so this should be taken into account when determining their structure and wording.

The language of such texts is generally adjusted to the subject being discussed and often-said language is quite technical. The author of this kind of writing should possess proven knowledge and show the reader that the book is based upon reliable and highly documented sources At the same time, the writer must be able to convey the information in a way that carefully balances the very technical nature of the information with its understandability for the reader.

The theme of these books cover a broad spectrum that can range from science to technology to legal, administrative, religious, psychological, etc.

## Literary

In the dictionary we can find the definition of literature as "art that employs words as the tool of creation." Although, when we write any kind of text we also use words as tools, literature seeks to create beauty with language. This term is being used here to encompass all other works of written art although all of the preceding could be included as literary styles.

The style and subsequent subsets are more deeply flourished with descriptive, colorful, and tangential artistic or literary license. Here is where color, taste, smell, sound, and touch meet feeling, hopes, and dreams. Whereas the preceding styles were much more directed at conveying facts and figures, possibly even using the "who", "what", "where", "when", "how" and "why" questions of reporting, the literary styles now being presented incorporate "for what reason", "why did they think this way", "why were they feeling this way" and explore the emotional interrelations of characters, time, and space. This is not only where the grass is greener but also speckled with yellow happy dandelions, smells of fresh clippings, drenched with cold dew, and waves gently in the warm breeze as if a thousand small arms were waving hello. Time is transcended, characters wander into memories, and hearts beat strongly from the pulse of the pentameter.

On this basis, we can make a distinction between other writing styles and those that we define as literary texts: fiction and nonfiction.

## Fiction

In a work of fiction, the author narrates imaginary events with fictional characters in order to entertain the reader. There are no limits in fiction; anything is possible in such creations, however, fact that it is imaginary does not impede the author from using elements of reality to compose his literary creation. Many famous novels were created from personal experiences of the authors. We all have interesting experiences that with the adequate embellishment and the right words can become quite a pleasure to readers.

The range of shapes that fiction can take is vast. From novels, stories, short stories, legends, poetry, fables. In short, the possibilities are endless.

**Write Now!** *From head to read in 90 days!*

If you have not yet decided where to begin, here are some of the themes that you can develop

| | |
|---|---|
| **Religion** | **Nautical** |
| **Drama** | **Novels** |
| **Eroticism** | **Cultures** |
| **Folklore** | **Poetry** |
| **Mythology** | **Romance** |
| **History** | **Fantasy** |
| **Mystery** | **Military** |
| **Crime** | **Cowboys** |
| **Esoteric** | **World** |

## Nonfiction

Nonfiction books are based on real information, which can be validated, verified, proven. Usually this type of text is based on a real event or is a product of the experiences of the author.

The most common forms of nonfiction are memoirs, biographies, autobiographies, essays and chronicles.

## Drafting/Layout

The kind of book you are writing and the audience it is aimed toward will set the tone for how the text will be drafted. You do not use the same language in a self-help book, which is designed to be read by people seeking easily digestible information, as that which you would use in a manual for engineers or accountants.

The writing and illustration in a book are key tools to capture the attention of your reader and the best way to organize and express your ideas. The use of illustrations is important. We recall a time when we were in a bookstore with a friend who was in indecisive about which book to buy, so within the store category he was flipping through pages very quickly without reading and he said, "Pictures, charts and diagrams have always attracted me more than just words."

And that's very true. This is essential in technical books, where the reader is looking to better learn the information with use of summary table or helpful illustrations.

Note that here the judgment and creativity of the author come into play. Maybe your subject requires photographs, drawings or maybe it your book is better served by simply titles, words and chapter headings as in a work of fiction.

There is no perfect recipe, but there are guidelines to follow that we use with our students when they are in the process of creating content. One of the main objectives in your layout should be clarity. We all want our message to be clear to anyone who reads our book. The best way is to write text that is easy to understand. To be clear we must handle the language well and respect grammar, spelling and syntax according to the standards within the language we are writing.

Another thing you must practice to write clearly is to avoid using complex words or convoluted ideas with the misconception that it will give your writing class. Clear text must avoid ambiguity. What we write should leave no doubt as to what we meant. Often you have to re-read what you wrote to ensure this. If, when you do this, you notice the slightest possibility that it can be misunderstood, then it is time to sit down and write the idea again.

The choice of the right words and the proper use of punctuation will be the first step towards achieving the goal of having the reader read it in the manner you imagined. A misplaced comma can express an idea that is totally contrary to the one that you sought to express.

In writing we must avoid duplication of words, seeking to avoid redundancy, and trying not to make unnecessary detours to express the idea. Although part of the charm of literature is in the use of metaphors and other poetic licenses, everything must be done with full awareness and proper choice of words to avoid falling into that abyss of works that ultimately express nothing.

When we decide to write a manuscript, we have to decide the features that we want it to have and keep it the same throughout. Only then we will achieve a consistent result. If we decide that our text will be written in the past tense, such as in a novel, we must be careful in the use of tenses and make sure that throughout the writing, it is clear that the actions are happening in the past.

It is the same with the use of person ($1^{st}$, $2^{nd}$, $3^{rd}$). If our text is a first-person narrative, we must maintain that feature constantly. Another great examples of this is if we are designing a manual like this and we decide to speak to the reader very informally by using contractions (you're, we're, etc.), we should not then begin speaking more traditionally to the reader by not using them. Our voice and style should be consistent throughout the manuscript.

## Editing

No book should be published without first passing through the hands of an editor (copyeditor, proofreader, style editor; in short, many names are given). Although the writer reviews the manuscript again and again it will always lack that look of a finished product if not reviewed by an editor, whose job it is to find those details that can be improved or corrected.

While many find it hard to believe, books of all known writers have passed through the hands of an editor before seeing the light of day. It is an unavoidable necessity, since many times the idea is original and needs to be very well structured; one little detail can make it fail to reach the reader.

Even if the writer is considered an expert in the use of language, an external look is required. The reason that this is so necessary is because when a person has worked a long time on his or her work, he or she loses objectivity when judging and this makes him or her blind to errors. Another reason is that the book, in many ways, becomes a part of the writer to the point that the two cannot be separated, making it impossible to read it from the perspective of the reader.

In the publishing world today, with the ease of using technology to self-publish, thousands of books are released every day, but only the extraordinary will be able to stand out in this sea of pages. With these kinds of odds, we cannot afford to skip this last vital step that allows you to escape any syntax errors, inappropriate conjugation or a comma out of place that can really affect the readability for readers.

Manuscript editing is the final look to correct the fine details of a work such as spelling, punctuation, consistency, coherence, structure, data correlation, possible contradictions within the text, the proper use of dialogue, the use of elements such as quotation marks, dashes, italics, among many other aspects that are part of this delicate task.

You might think that you have this problem solved with use of a word processor, but let us say that unfortunately these programs are of very little help when it comes to making the text flawless. In fact, there are many times that you could thoughtlessly accept the changes recommended and be putting errors into your work and not the other way around.

It is important that the content of the book that you are thinking of writing is your first priority. Once you think you have captured the idea that you had in mind and have reviewed it to assure that you have left nothing out and that your book is coherent and well sequenced, it will be time to turn to the experts who are dedicated to cleaning and polishing what will be your masterpiece.

Within the range of services we provide in 90daysoulmate we obviously found ourselves proofreading and correcting, but through this experience we have found that the author may lose inspiration if, at the time of writing, he or she must be preoccupied with grammar and punctuation. The idea is that the final product is not only a source of pride for you, but that it is appreciated and well accepted by the greatest number of readers.

Write Now! *From head to read in 90 days!*

**Notes**

## Chapter IX

## Cover design

The cover plays an important role in the presentation of your book: it is the way that you capture a reader with no more than a single glance. We could relate that well-known phrase that <u>you do not choose a book; the book chooses you</u>. When you visit a bookstore or do a search on a web page for a book on a specific topic, a lot of times the choice is based on what it looks like, hopefully love at first sight. Only after being intrigued by the cover, do we open it up to read a little sample to see if it is worth our time.

That first successful impact is due to an attractive cover, specific to the type of reader that the *"book decides to choose"*. That is when the reader, perhaps without much thought at all, takes the book in his hands and carries it home.

That is why we recommend that you seek professional help to design the cover, because although you have in your mind the idea of what you want, many experts can polish that idea and bring it to a more professional level in order to present book that is attractive in every way.

It is the job of the designer to play with colors, images, fonts, organization and symmetry, based on the audience you want to reach.

In our research, we have photographed shelves full of books. We then ask a group of people to choose from approximately 200 designs. It is amazing how a select number of the colors and designs are very popular and chosen a majority of the time.

Earlier we discussed who is your reader, or the demographics of your audience. Your title should scream their name, or give a distinct benefit or result they will get from reading the book, or be a title easy to remember or associate with the subject matter. A romance novel entitled only <u>Rita</u> with a blank cover will draw a different audience than a book entitled <u>Rita's Spicy Italian Discovery</u>. Imagine the latter with a picture of a characteristically tall, dark, and handsome Italian gondolier closely embracing a woman along the waterways of Venice as they shimmer in an evening sky (both Venice and the couple).

## Images

As discussed, the images are very important for attracting attention to the cover and attempting to gain your audience's interest. The images placed on the front, back and inside the book should be owned or purchased. You must be careful that you are correctly using copyrighted materials.

Sometimes our clients provide their own images, but lack the necessary resolution for good printing and reproduction for books in different formats. That is why we recommend that you obtain a high quality image and, above all, establish a style. If, for example, you are using cartoons as illustrations in some chapters, keep the same approach in the rest of the book. Do mix styles of pictures or mix color photos with black and white, or sepia-tone, etc.

Strive for consistency and harmony of content in all of your images. The same applies to the use of diagrams, tables, graphs, which should be designed with the same style, taking special care with the lettering font, size, colors, etc.

## Titles & Subtitles

The title of a book should be thought of no less than naming your newborn son. The name should be attractive, representing the content you want to publish. It should be easy to remember, and you should especially try to be unique, because using a title of a book that already exists can bring many problems. Finding a good name is an arduous task. We recommend that you create a list of possible options and then you verify if there is a book with the same title. Once your list is verified you can ask your friends for feedback, or place it on your social network, or any means that allows you to select an ideal title consistent with the idea that your book represents.

The subtitles are as important, or perhaps even more important, than the title itself; they are the best way to explain in short sentences what your book is to get the attention of the reader. When you establish a subtitle, this may allow you to adjust your original title, so you must be flexible in adjusting and changing until the last moment. You should use catchy phrases that complement the title, to draw the reader to the book either because it looks like interesting information or because of simple curiosity. This is a task of professional marketing.

In some cases the subtitle we recommend using sentences that begin with "how," "when," "why" for emphasis, function or focus on the idea you want to express in your work. This is especially true for non-fiction whereas the benefit of reading the book must be readily apparent from a quick glance at the cover.

For example let us look at our first book, titled: *Single?* That seems to be a title that draws attention to those who are single, but there is more behind it. There is a complementing subtitle: *How I found my perfect match in 90 days.* That phrase tells you that the idea of the book is finding your perfect match in 90 days. Such subtitles challenge the reader who is simply browsing to actually open it up and take look, whether married or not, to see what it is all about. Their response to the subtitle might be, "Oh yeah? Prove it to me!" We also decided to put more information on the front cover to entice the casual browser to easily take a closer look if they so inclined.

In another example, let us look at our second book. There we put two subtitles to explain more about the content. The title is: *90 Day*

*Challenge*. The first subtitle reads: *How to get the results you want in just 90 days*. Then at the bottom of the cover, it is complemented by a second sentence, which reads: *A day-by-day method to your own successful business.*

Plus we also added: *Instantly change your focus and see what you can be...* This tied into our company motto and since we use the book at our seminars and workshops we use the book as a brochure, workbook, and promotional piece. Three in one!

In the case of novels or stories simply a title is enough, but it must be very attractive. Perhaps when the author's name is famous it requires no more information, otherwise, even here you may want a catchy one-liner to draw readers to your book.

Our books tend to be non-fiction, self-help, and workbook or textbook style. The main point is that the book should serve its purpose for its intended audience. Out style is what we have chosen to go to market with because of how it ties in with our businesses, workshops, and publicity platforms.

Write Now!                    *From head to read in 90 days!*

A selection of covers produced for various clients where we either purchased artwork with rights or were provided artwork by the client. The cover layouts we produced were for a number of psychologists and authors with therapeutic or self-help missions. Messages were congruent with subject matter. The focuses were children, families, therapy, psychology, and relationships.

6" X 9" Paperbacks

100-130 Pages

*Challenge*. The first subtitle reads: *How to get the results you want in just 90 days*. Then at the bottom of the cover, it is complemented by a second sentence, which reads: *A day-by-day method to your own successful business.*

Plus we also added: *Instantly change your focus and see what you can be...* This tied into our company motto and since we use the book at our seminars and workshops we use the book as a brochure, workbook, and promotional piece. Three in one!

In the case of novels or stories simply a title is enough, but it must be very attractive. Perhaps when the author's name is famous it requires no more information, otherwise, even here you may want a catchy one-liner to draw readers to your book.

Our books tend to be non-fiction, self-help, and workbook or textbook style. The main point is that the book should serve its purpose for its intended audience. Out style is what we have chosen to go to market with because of how it ties in with our businesses, workshops, and publicity platforms.

# Write Now! *From head to read in 90 days!*

6" X 9" Paperback

130 Pages

Write Now! *From head to read in 90 days!*

8" X 10" Paperback

216 Pages

Write Now!  *From head to read in 90 days!*

A selection of covers produced for various clients where we either purchased artwork with rights or were provided artwork by the client. The cover layouts we produced were for a number of psychologists and authors with therapeutic or self-help missions. Messages were congruent with subject matter. The focuses were children, families, therapy, psychology, and relationships.

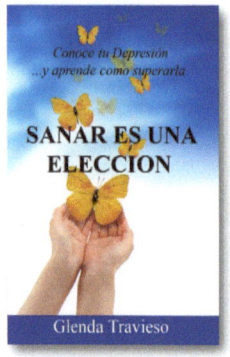

6" X 9" Paperbacks

100-130 Pages

We took what we learned from our cover development activities to produce the cover for *90 Day Soulmate*. Each cover project is a custom work and needing to be developed with audience, content, and author personality in mind.

6" X 9" Paperback

130 Pages

## Author Bio

Depending on the type of book you want to write or are already writing, including the biography is an important point for the reader. You need to do this in all cases at the time of registering the book. Publishers are interested to knowing who is the author of the work.

Often in stories and novels, they do not include the biography of the author in the manuscript; in other cases such as nonfiction, research, technical information, guides, history, etc. it is absolutely imperative.

The biography should be condensed, expressing highlights from your career, both professionally and personally. Just because a client writes self help books does not mean that he or she is a psychologist or therapist. His or her work experience and life of helping others has given him or her the ability to write a book. So we recommend including these experiences, so that the reader understands the value of information through the writer's experience.

Some people like to add a photo of the author, so that the reader has an idea of what the author looks like. By being more open about who you are, you can attract more followers. Otherwise you could go unnoticed in this vast world of writers.

The biography can be placed on the back cover or on the inside of the book, either at the beginning or end. The organization of information in the biography should instill confidence in the author on the part of the reader and generate a lot of interest in reading the book.

## Back cover and spine

In the back of the book you should compliment the information included in your book, either in short phrases, images, or from recommendations from others that you want to highlight in order to make what your book is about very clear to readers.

It is important to maintain the harmony of the design between the front and back covers such that the reader is invited to easily travel across the book with colors, letters and images that suggest continuity. Remember to leave room for the ISBN, which is the registration number of your book, as well as the bar code.

Depending on the number of pages contained in your book, evaluate the information that you placed in the back of it. If it is too thin, we do not recommend writing anything on the spine, but if you suitable space on the spine, you should place the title and your name. We do suggest that you make the book large enough to house identification on the spine. This may be the only part of the book seen if your fortunate to have your book carried by bookstores and libraries.

Write Now!                                          *From head to read in 90 days!*

Example of our bio and back cover of the business oriented book:

**90 Day Solutions, LLC.**
90 DaySolutions LLC., provides audits, employee training, recommendations for process improvement, and documentation of quality management systems. Since 2000, it has provided consulting services to more than seventy (70) companies in the list of the top 500 world-class companies. Clients have included energy, gas, oil, automotive, healthcare, manufacturing, food, education, government, financial services, and telecommunications industries. The variety of customers has spread throughout the world, from small businesses with private operations to large multinational companies. Many clients wish to obtain ISO (International Standard Organization) certification in management systems, while others endeavor to develop a clear vision, define the mission of the business, uncover their unique strategy to success, motivate employees, and accomplish new goals through transformational leadership.

**Lisett Guevara**
Lisett Guevara, has achieved a Doctorate in Education Science, Masters in Industrial Engineering, and Bachelor of Science in Information Engineering. She has over 20 years of university teaching experience at the undergraduate and graduate levels; led and implemented educational projects on subjects such as teamwork, rules of negotiating, and effective communication; and implemented strategies to uncover untapped effectiveness in

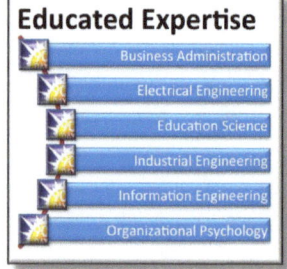

people. Since 1998, Lisett has established herself as an expert business consultant, coach, and mentor, helping more than 200 companies and 1,500 couples and individuals.

**Jim Gulnick**
Since graduating with a Bachelor of Science in Electrical Engineering in 1988, Jim Gulnick has developed a deep and broad experience in business operations, finance, sales, marketing, and training within public and private companies across numerous specialized industries. Jim has a Masters in Business Administration with an educational journey that culminates towards a Ph.D. in Industrial and Organizational Psychology. Jim combines the logical processes of business operations with the powerful art of marketing and psychology.

*See what you can be.*
90daysolutions.com

Here the company and its services are more fully explored as well as the expertise brought to the table. Remember, if your book is your calling card or used in your business, it is also a place to market your services. The spine is shown on the right.

Write Now! *From head to read in 90 days!*

In this example of our book dealing with relationship, our back cover includes a more intimate and less formal feel:

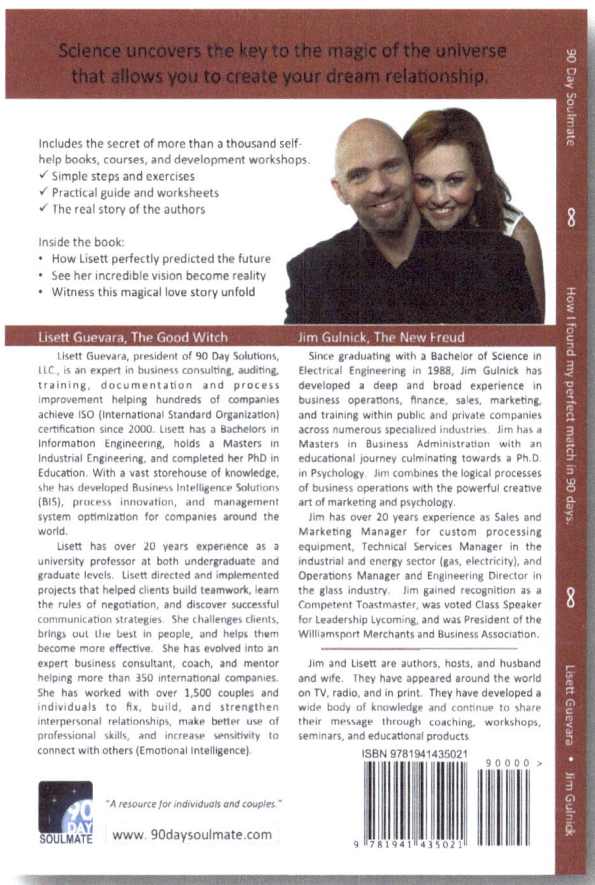

The picture indicates our close relationship and yet we are still able to promote what's inside the book and provide details about our backgrounds with our bios. The spine is shown on the right.

## Type of covers

The most common covers on the market are classified as:

1. – Soft cover

 ⇒ Glued or Welded

 ⇒ Stapled

 ⇒ Spiral

2. – Hard cover

 ⇒ Glued or welded (simple)

 ⇒ Glued or welded (glossy)

 ⇒ Spiral

**Notes**

Write Now!           *From head to read in 90 days!*

# Chapter X

## Registering your copyright

In this part you should be very careful, because you will give your book to a publisher or publishing company, and we have known cases of fraudulent organizations, who, after you have delivered the manuscript and registration money, simply vanish.

But on the flipside of this, sometimes we, as publishers, get materials which, according to the author, are ready to be published, but at the time of review by our team of professionals, we notice that the material is referencing information that belongs to others without proper approval from the owner, the content is confusing, or that there are problems of grammar and spelling, etc. In these cases, we offer some content services, based upon what the author needs.

In the case of a publishing company, when you give them your content, they are simply approving or denying their services in the publishing of the book. It takes in some cases months of waiting, often without even knowing if the company is legitimate or not, just to have your manuscript returned a time later at which time you have to start this process all over again.

*Copyright* is a process for protecting your content under the laws of the country in which you want to register your work. They must be original works of authorship, including literary, dramatic, musical, artistic, etc. The law grants copyright ownership of exclusive rights to the author or the ability to authorize others, in part or in full, to take over various elements of the management of the book.

When you deliver your document to a publisher or publishing company, they perform the registration of copyright and, depending on the agreement established with them, will record who has exclusive rights to the content and to what extent.

In other cases you may want to establish copyright by yourself, if you are interested in publishing the work yourself. If so, you must perform a series of steps that can be done electronically or physically, filling in the required information, the payment of the prescribed fee, the registration fees and the presentation of the work in the required formats

## Getting an ISBN

The ISBN is a unique international identification number for publications. Thus, this unique number prevents copying errors and classifies the content and format, whether print or digital, as well as the content type, style cover, etc.

A book should be assigned an ISBN for publication. It cannot be sold in a bookstore, printed, or published as a digital document for electronic devices without having a specific ISBN. This is acquired through an agency that legally assigns an ISBN number. Others buy in bulk and sell or supply when they publish the book for the author. Typically we buy in bulk because it is far less expensive if you are publishing multiple books per year.

This ISBN code allows the updating of databases and directories of books internationally for easy classification, location and marketing. When performing an ISBN purchase, we simply provide a number generated by the system, depending on the classification of the text. Subsequently, we must make the number into a barcode for easy digital scanning at store checkout. All marketing and selling is done through this code. Then, depending on the agreement that you establish with the publishing company, you will start to receive income from the sale of your book.

In the event that your work is published in both paper and digital formats, you must establish a different ISBN number for each version. In the case of books that will be sold in different countries, it is important to check the conditions of each country, if the same number applies, or if you need a new number for that particular country. You must take all conditions into account when establishing your market strategy and to determine where to distribute your book.

Every time the book is published in a new way (for example: Spanish vs. English), a new copyright and a new ISBN are required. The latter must be included in the presentation of the book at the copyright office. We usually simultaneously obtain or assign an ISBN and register copyright. This can all be done electronically through ISBN providers and the Electronic Copyright Office (eCO).

For this part, we recommend that you seek the assistance of experts in the field. There is also a lot of material on the Internet that can help you to understand the different requirements for registering your work. The picture below shows the bottom right corner of one of our books and the location of the ISBN and barcode signifying the unique identification mark for this published work. The barcode includes the ISBN and pricing identification. Where the 9 0 0 0 0 is located is typically the price of the book at full retail. The 13 digit ISBN appears to the left.

**Notes**

Write Now! *From head to read in 90 days!*

## Chapter XI

### Publishing your book

We can give you many options when it comes to publishing, from looking for a publishing company to self-publishing. There are different ways to get your book published, three of which are: professional publishing, vanity publishing and self-publishing, among others.

A professional publisher, also called a traditional or commercial publisher, accepts few manuscripts and usually does not allow unsolicited submissions. Unknown authors can wait months to finally hear the rejection and quite possibly not receive any comments.

If what you want is the quick publication of your manuscript by a publisher, then you will likely be constantly calling or sending emails to a literary agent, who will probably put you in touch with what is known as a vanity publisher. They will make sure your book is printed, but this is a higher priced alternative in which the company will tell you that your manuscript is good and then they will sell you a legal agreement or contract regarding the proceeds of your book. They show you how it works with a couple of little-known authors who achieved a good amount of successful sales and promise you the opportunity to work with the same team for a fixed price. Many of these companies help to get the copyright of your book and the ISBN.

But wait, they get these rights on their behalf and therefore they possess the book and give you just a small portion of sales. These firms will definitely get your book published, but they leave you on your own after the book is printed, making you responsible for the marketing of your book.

Many authors are turning to <u>self-publishing</u> after having no success with publishers and reading the critical reviews of the publishing houses. In self-publishing the author is responsible for editing, creating a cover, formatting, obtaining copyrights and ISBN, and finding a printing service on demand. This is the low cost solution once you've been through the experience of trial and error.

There is a hybrid solution called <u>hybrid-publishing</u>. This is when a professional organization for a fee helps make you a self-publishing author. Such organizations provide training services and guidelines to authors, assist in cover development, revisions and editing, and hand carried to the authors through all the processes for publication.

The latter is the concept we perfected in 90daysoulmate.com, LLC. We promote giving freedom to our clients to place their book directly on Amazon and available for sale in bookstore and numerous channels. The author has the direct ability to track sales. This element sets us apart from many other publishing organizations. One disadvantage is that the author must perform the marketing of his or her own book. We simply prepare and make the book available for publication, sales management, and distribution control by the author. Plus, there is no share in the profits that the author must distribute.

We know it is not easy selling a book on a large scale. In this time when you already have your book nearly ready, let us inform you that you will need to put as much or more effort toward marketing as you did writing the book. But do not be discouraged; we just want you to be aware about the new challenges that you will face from that point after the book is ready, recorded, and published. The new challenges to market your book will take the same discipline that you had to have to write it.

Deciding to deliver your book to a publishing company and negotiate rights may be a more convenient way, because they take on the job of designing a promotion and distribution plan. This will greatly benefit you because they will make your book available in many places. But the fact that you dropped the manuscript off with a publisher does not mean you should just sit and wait for results. Your advocacy, and advertising should be deliberate and continual from that moment on.

Customers with whom we have worked have developed many promotional ideas: creating seminars, attending radio and TV interviews, holding book signings and events in libraries, paying public relations firms to promote their media image, free promotional items, etc.

There are many ways to promote and, as noted in Chapter VI when you understand who your reader is, you can develop strategies that enable you to establish an effective marketing plan in which the most important thing is working smarter, not harder, by having a good plan rather than investing a lot of time and money without one.

In order for your promotion to be effective, it is important that you have your book in different formats such as audio, digital and paper. The fact that people can hear your book while driving or they can buy online and read on an electronic device makes you more versatile. The more products you have, the more opportunities you have to penetrate different types of markets.

This transition by the world of writers leaves us with the feeling that the authors have developed and established a legacy, a mark that is unique and can help many. Under this concept you should reflect on your promotion. You must make your audience feel that you are making a contribution, providing assistance that, in one way or another, will be re-paid.

Sometimes we have even gone as far as giving a book away for possibly a seminar or event to open up the possibilities of becoming more well known. We invite you to play in the wonderful world of being a writer looking to share your message as it ***challenges your creativity and discipline to achieve recognition.***

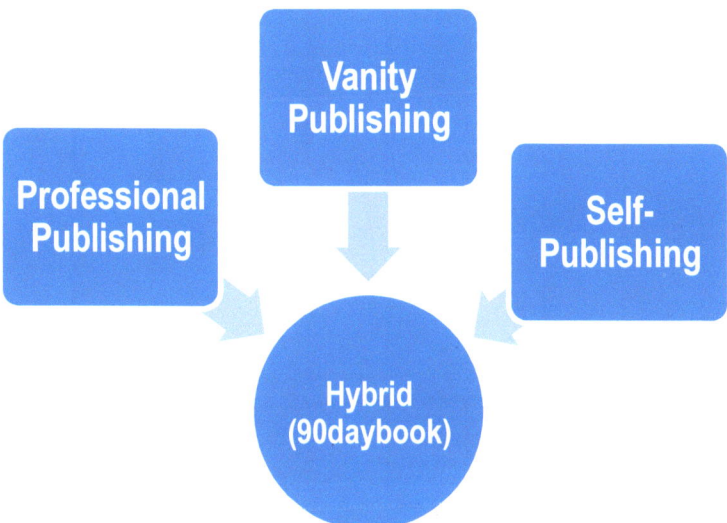

Write Now! *From head to read in 90 days!*

## Chapter XII

### Establishing your 90 day plan

Every project has a plan. The fact that inspiration strikes unexpectedly according to many artists does not mean you should not make a plan to organize and discipline your inspiration. Developing a plan allows you to sprint rather than crawl down the road toward the goal of being a well-known author, because you know the steps you need to follow to take necessary actions along the way; also, it will help you realize when you have deviated from your plan. **Time management, discipline to devote to the project and being focused on your goals are the key tools for the success of your book.** We want to give this recipe, step by step, so that you achieve that which has so hindered your ability to get everything you want out of life.

This plan has been implemented again and again and has been very successful in meeting the goal of completing and publishing a book in just 90 days. So without further ado, please view the chart on the next page and know that you can fill it out and adjust it to meet your needs. This book is designed for between 120 and 200 pages ... and this can be accomplished in the time allotted. Breaking the necessary work down into activities requiring chunks of effort split over time makes it possible to methodically and energetically approach book writing. Your book will be from head to read in 90 days!

# Write Now! From head to read in 90 days!

## 90 Day Plan to Write Your Book

| DAY | Activity | Week 1 | 2 | 3 | 4 | 5 | 6 | 7 | 8 | 9 | 10 | 11 | 12 | 13 |
|---|---|---|---|---|---|---|---|---|---|---|---|---|---|---|
| 1 | Define your and your book's mission | ■ | | | | | | | | | | | | |
| 5 | Develop your 90 day plan | ■ | | | | | | | | | | | | |
| 10 | Connecting with your audience | | ■ | | | | | | | | | | | |
| 11 | Define your legacy | | ■ | | | | | | | | | | | |
| 12 | Connect your skills with your book | | ■ | | | | | | | | | | | |
| 12 | What resources do you have? | | ■ | | | | | | | | | | | |
| 14 | Determine your limits | | ■ | | | | | | | | | | | |
| 15 | Determine your target reader/market | | | ■ | | | | | | | | | | |
| 17 | Match emotional style of book with reader | | | ■ | | | | | | | | | | |
| 18 | Develop attraction list | | | ■ | | | | | | | | | | |
| 19 | Select the style of writing | | | ■ | | | | | | | | | | |
| 19 | Basic structure of the content, DELIVERY 1st Chapter | | | ■ | | | | | | | | | | |
| 20 | Development 2 chapters and their revision and analysis (1,2,3) | | | ■ | | | | | | | | | | |
| 28 | Send to review organization and content | | | | ■ | | | | | | | | | |
| 30 | Development 2 chapters and their revision and analysis (4,5) | | | | ■ | | | | | | | | | |
| 30 | Send to review organization and content | | | | ■ | | | | | | | | | |
| 35 | Development 2 chapters and their revision and analysis (6,7) | | | | | ■ | | | | | | | | |
| 40 | Send to review organization and content | | | | | ■ | | | | | | | | |
| 45 | Development 2 chapters and their revision and analysis (8,9) | | | | | | ■ | | | | | | | |
| 45 | Send to review organization and content | | | | | | ■ | | | | | | | |
| 55 | Development 2 chapters and their revision and analysis (10, prefasio) | | | | | | | ■ | | | | | | |
| 60 | Send to review organization and content | | | | | | | | ■ | | | | | |
| 65 | Send to review spelling and grammar | | | | | | | | | ■ | | | | |
| 70 | Send corrections and reorganzation of | | | | | | | | | ■ | | | | |
| 75 | Check for need of revision | | | | | | | | | | ■ | | | |
| 75 | Send to two friends for feedback | | | | | | | | | | ■ | | | |
| 78 | Prepare the cover concept | | | | | | | | | | | ■ | | |
| 78 | Select the images and title | | | | | | | | | | | ■ | | |
| 80 | Prepare cover and biography for publication | | | | | | | | | | | ■ | | |
| 85 | Submit and establish copyright | | | | | | | | | | | | ■ | |
| 86 | Secure an ISBN | | | | | | | | | | | | ■ | |
| 86 | Convert ISBN to bar code for cover with pricing | | | | | | | | | | | | ■ | |
| 87 | Register on POD website to publish | | | | | | | | | | | | ■ | |
| 88 | Upload cover and description to POD service | | | | | | | | | | | | | ■ |
| 90 | Choose sales channels | | | | | | | | | | | | | ■ |

## Day 1: Define your and your book's mission

To follow this plan, take a look at the activities you must perform each day. On day 1 you must define your mission and your book's mission. There, you simply write what you consider your life's mission and your book's missions to be.

## Day 5: Develop your 90 day plan

Simply make a plan similar to the preceding table, but adjusted to the size of your book, for example, Day 20's activities (developing two chapters per week) may vary if your book has over 200 pages and twelve chapters. Then, you make adjustments so that Day 30's activities (write the other chapters) can be aligned with your target.

## Day 10: Who is your reader?

Here you must do some preliminary work on the exercise in Chapter VI to begin to understand your audience. It is only with knowledge of your reader that you will be able to customize the content and writing style to match the interest and desires of your audience. This is a powerful way to begin your adventure of connection.

## Days 11-12: Define your legacy, Connect your skills with your book, and What resources do you have?

What is your legacy? Refer back to Chapter III where possibly you made notes and try to pinpoint this, based on the mission you set and the legacy you want to leave. With these notes and knowing your reader you can better connect with whom you want help, reach, or impact with your book.

Chapter VII helps you determine your skills to connect the book you want to write with your audience. It is with this that you will develop the material for the following days. You will need to determine your competencies and how best to use them to connect with others.

Also, look back also at your exercise "Taking action on your ideas" where you used the mental map and you described the areas you want to develop. On Day 12 check the resources available to you. Describe them very well, because you are going to use them to both develop your book and to sell it. It is important to have this document always visible in your place of inspiration, so that you remember the way you should go.

| Areas | Resources | How to connect them |
|---|---|---|
| | | |
| | | |
| | | |
| | | |
| | | |

## Day 14: Determine your limits

What are you afraid of? It is time to address and create the self-sabotaging blacklist. It will be important that you also have it on hand as you proceed with your 90-day plan. The moment those sabotaging ghosts appear, you just review the list of what you fear, and those ghosts disappear. We conduct exercises in our seminar where the participants first develop a list of the things that they fear might inhibit the development of their book. Then columns are added in which "why" and "when" are added for more specificity. And finally, "how to reduce fear" is decided. It is amazing how just by facing those ghosts they lose their power to sabotage your project.

| Self-Sabotaging Black List ||||
|---|---|---|---|
| Things that scare you | Why? | When? | How do you reduce your fear? |
| | | | |
| | | | |
| | | | |
| | | | |
| | | | |
| | | | |
| | | | |

Write Now!                  *From head to read in 90 days!*

| Things that scare you | Why? | When? | How do you reduce your fear? |
|---|---|---|---|
|  |  |  |  |
|  |  |  |  |

Self-Sabotage is what holds us back from achieving many of our goals in life. Some items are innate and others are programs from our families, friends, religion, culture, and environment. Creating your future starts with distilling your past and breaking through self-imposed limitations.

## Day 15: Determine your target reader/market

Determining who your reader is, is well explained in Chapter VI. Describe each piece of information that is indicated in this chapter. Some people assume they know the answers and do not fill in the information. We recommend that you write, and write, and write some more. It is the best way to see the information you have. You forget things faster than you think. The information in your mind is likely to be forgotten, or change in seconds. Unless you actually write down your ideas, you risk just being a dreamer who never really gets anything done.

Raise your hand, make a fist, and shout, "I am in control of my future by being in control of my present!" Write now! It is your choice.

## Day 17-18: Match emotional style of book with reader and Develop attraction list

Based on the type of reader and how you connected this with your skills, it will be possible to determine the emotions that you can use to make your book addictive to the reader. You can create a list of elements that make your book attractive, and get to know what your style is. Talk to your audience, in your voice, straightforward or colorfully, in your style – the style that meets your audience where they live, with your content, and combined with the skills you possess for connection. In our case, we use exercises, charts and graphs, and talk informally with a mix of styles, formatting, and examples.

## Day 19: Select your style of writing and Basic structure of the content

With all the data organized, at this moment, you must set a schematic structure, which consists of drafting tentative chapter headings that you are going to develop as you write. Remember that both the title of the book as the chapters may change along the way as your book develops. And we always recommend that the final title not be decided upon until designing your cover as the two go hand in hand as the face of your book to the world. We added elements to our cover to match our audience as well as draw upon our *90 Day Soulmate* branding strategy.

## Day 20-30: Develop chapters, revise, and analyze, and Review content and organization

It is time to write your first chapter. Here you must dedicate yourself solely to writing, regardless of grammar or spelling. It is time to get inspired and write whatever comes to mind. At the end of a few pages, return to the start and begin to clean the redundancy, correct spelling, add words and check your punctuation. At the conclusion of the first chapter, review it a couple times and then send it to a proofreader, who will help you make necessary adjustments.

This is where you start your pace for completing your work in the time you have planned. Break down the work by day and keep on track. This is where structure meets creativity. A strong start gets you going right out of the gate.

## Day 30-60: Develop chapters, revise, and analyze, and Review content and organization (continue moving forward)

We recommend maintaining the momentum of work daily in your book. Set a strict schedule to concentrate and produce. If you spend 3 to 4 hours daily to finish your book, we guarantee you can finish within 90 days. Maintaining writing discipline, revising, editing and adjusting give you the chance to advance to the next chapter. After completing each chapter you will review everything, without interruption, to determine repeated elements, jumps in time, lack of information or excess of it.

## Day 60: Send to review organization and content

Correction on the back end involves reviewing all elements of grammar, spelling and any other details that may distract or annoy the reader. At this point, you should seek support from someone else, because you have written and read your own content more than five or six times, and it is difficult for you to catch everything. Get support from a professional or perhaps a friend who is a good reader and can provide you with this back end correction.

## Day 65: Send to review spelling and grammar

Review the book several times again and then send the whole book to be reviewed by another, asking them to consider the form and substance of your book. In this case, spelling and grammar are the specific focus of review.

## Day 70-75: Send corrections and reorganization of chapters if needed, Check for need of revision, and Send to two friends for feedback

Make any further corrections to organization, content, spelling, and grammar. Do one more review of the shape of the book looking for flow and continuity of layout. Shape correction refers to adjusting the size of texts chosen for the book format, including the titles of the chapters, font size, tables, charts, figures, any illustrations, footnotes, etc. Once reviewed thoroughly, send the book for one final external review of organization and content. By this time, the book should have been reviewed multiple times by multiple people enabling you to have confidence in your work.

## Day 78: Prepare the cover concept and Select images and title

Within preparing your cover concept relies upon clear identification of the market to which you are going to direct your book with use of attraction gaining images, colors, fonts, etc. Remember that the cover is very important when you submit your book. I always remember the phrase that people do not choose a book, but the book chooses them. This refers to seeing a series of books on a shelf in a bookstore; you notice one by its cover. Then, not knowing what is inside, take the book, try it out a little and then you will wear it. The cover is a key element in this moment of attraction.

Search images, whether they are purchased or designed, and write sentences that help you capture the attention and summarize all the ideas in your book, if possible, in ten words. Here, it is also important to seek professional help, because designers are very creative people who have more experience in this field. In the case of doing it yourself, you rely on the information of the previous chapter on designing the cover.

The cover images attract. The title, subtitle and other cover content create further interest and desire. The table of contents and chapters create increased desire. If you have matched your content to your target utilizing your skills of connection, then you have the best chance of triggering an emotional reaction resulting in a purchase.

## Day 80: Prepare cover and biography for publication

Finalize cover, spine, and biography and save as PDF formatted for future uploading to print-on-demand (POD) service. At this point the book itself should be in finalized format and ready to convert into PDF.

## Day 85: Submit and establish copyright

Assemble your cover with the text of your book in the recommended formats for the publication. Depending on the type of publication you want, whether on paper, digital or audiobook. You must have the cover design and content ready to be uploaded into a publication app or system. It is important to build the document with links to chapters and an index for easy use and access. Prepare the text in PDF format to be uploaded to the portal. Establish copyright through electronic copyright office registration and submittal of PDF document.

## Day 86: Secure an ISBN and Convert ISBN to bar code for cover with pricing information

Once you have the registration of copyright, ISBN registration starts.

This registration number must be made into a barcode to place on the back of your book. Day 80 through 90 meld together depending on how, where, and who is submitting material. Some POD services will obtain an ISBN for you but you will be responsible for obtaining copyright. We will not address all options at this point because depending on many factors the order of who does what when changes. I had to read that three times myself!

### Day 87: Register on POD website to publish and Upload cover, content, and description

Registering on the website where you want to publish your book requires time and expertise as the information put there determines the success of the classification and subsequent searches for your book.

Once registered on the publishing site, you must wait for verification and approval. If the cover or content has any issues such as size, resolution, sharpness, margins, spine format, etc., your information will be returned for review and adjustment. This will probably take a couple of days.

### Day 90: Choose sales channels

When your material is approved it may take between 48-72 hours to make it available on marketing pages. This is when you have just taken a giant leap into publishing, but at the same time it is the beginning of a new process. It is time to establish a marketing plan that allows you to promote and sell your book.

If you are ready to create your own 90 Day Plan to Write Your Book and follow the steps in *Write Now!*, then we can congratulate you. We welcome you to enjoy this extraordinary world of inspiration where you will know the pleasure of creation and sharing the infinite resources of knowledge with Mankind. You are on an exciting journey of self-actualization as

*Remember that undocumented ideas are just dreams that fade in time!*

*Write Now!*

*www.90daybook.com*

Thank you for reading our book. We look forward to you using this material to bring your gifts to the world, inspire others, and share your talents.

Love,

Lisett and Jim